4Ruby

To my three diamonds Josh, Zac and Ben. You are the jewels in my crown.

May this work honour you Jesus, my Lord and my God.

"And the Word was made flesh and dwelt amongst us," John 1:14

Author's Note

This book is based on the Theology of The Body teachings of St Pope John Paul II, whose deep biblical insights continue to call people of all backgrounds into the very heart of the gospels.

The images and text in this book present the concepts of the Theology of The Body teachings specifically for little ones. *Jesus Had a Body Like Me* communicates the message of God's love to babies and the youngest of readers.

It is a call to love and be loved.

For a free audio version of this book, subscribe at:

https://www.subscribepage.com/d9i9n2

This flower is called the Lily of the Valley.

Did you know that it is sometimes used as a symbol for our friend Jesus? Sometimes it is also used as a symbol for our Mother Mary.

There is a Lily of the Valley hiding on every page. Can you find it?

God is Love.

That is why God made the world and He made you and me.

We are made of Love.

We are made in God's image ...

... and He gave us a beautiful body as a gift.

"Every good gift and every perfect gift is from above" Jas 1:17

He breathed into it ...

Whoooshh!

"But there is a spirit within people, the breath of the Almighty within them ..." Job 32:8

Our bodies can hold our feelings inside.

Our bodies can let our feelings out.

With our body we can explore the world around us ...

Our mouths can taste,
our nose can smell,
our eyes can see,
our skin can feel,
our ears can hear.

I am a girl like Mary. God gave me a girl's body.

My brother is a boy like Jesus. God gave him a boy's body.

You are special to God and He **loves** you so much ...

that Jesus came down from Heaven to be with His friends: you and me.

His body was just like ours.

Jesus taught us how to use our bodies

to love one another,

to help each other,

and be kind.

We can make things and we can play.

We can sing and we can pray.

Until one day we can all be together in God's **Love** forever.

In Heaven.

A prayer:

Jesus has no body but ours,

He has no hands but ours,

He has no feet but ours.

Our eyes are the ones that Jesus uses to look upon the world with kindness.

Our feet are the ones that Jesus uses to take us to others, to do good works.

Our hands are the ones that Jesus now uses to bless people.

Thank You God for my body. Amen

An adaptation of a prayer attributed to St Teresa of Avilla

Acknowledgements and further information

St. Pope John Paul II and the collection of his 129 catecheses on human love that were eventually compiled as *Man and Woman He Created Them: A Theology of the Body* (2006).

Illustrations by Kama Towcik.

Initial edits by Dr Lydia Saleh Rofail.

Faith in this project, countless revisions, in-house I.T. department, ongoing support, all of this and much more from my husband (the Yeti), and our cubs. This endeavour couldn't and wouldn't be without you!

Consistent bouts of encouragement by the remarkable women in our **Theology of the Body** forum: Angela, Chrissy, Doaa, Irene, Lydia, Margaret, Maria, Marie, Sheren, and Suzie.

Sister Anne Wood, OLSH, for introducing **Theology the Body** to me along with Christopher West's work. Almost 20 years ago, you sparked the flame that over time has set my heart on fire!

Christopher West, for inspiring me.

Mum, Dad, and Marie-Gloria, for giving me my first lessons in **love**.

To all the readers of *Jesus Had a Body Like Me*, young and not so young, thank YOU for buying this book!

† With every purchase of this book, a percentage of profits will be donated to The Sisters of Life who, in honour of Jesus their Bridegroom, defend and protect all life and continue to reflect His **Love** in our world.

Fisher, C 2021, Jesus Had a Body Like Me, Edition 1, Kinnereth Publishing, Sydney.

ISBN: 978-0-6451318-0-2 (eBook)
ISBN: 978-0-6451318-1-9 (print)

© 2021 Sydney, Australia

All rights reserved. No part of this book may be reproduced or modified in any form, including photocopying, recording, or by any information storage and retrieval system, without permission in writing from the publisher.

info@kinnereth.com.au

www.ingramcontent.com/pod-product-compliance
Lightning Source LLC
Chambersburg PA
CBHW041946110426
42744CB00027B/25